Guess What

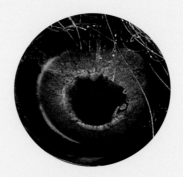

Published in the United States of America by
Cherry Lake Publishing
Ann Arbor, Michigan
www.cherrylakepublishing.com

Content Adviser: Susan Heinrichs Gray
Reading Adviser: Marla Conn MS, Ed., Literacy specialist, Read-Ability, Inc.
Book Designer: Felicia Macheske

Photo Credits: © Mr_seng/Shutterstock, cover; © Yatra/Shutterstock.com, 1, 4; © Panom/Shutterstock.com, 3; © Olga_i/
Shutterstock.com, 7; © jeep2499/Shutterstock.com, 8; © JONATHAN PLEDGER/Shutterstock.com, 11; © AppStock/Shutterstock.com,
12; © nimwsw/Shutterstock.com, 15; © MrWildLife/Shutterstock.com, 17; © Stephane Bidouze/Shutterstock.com 18; © ballykdy/
Shutterstock.com, 21; © Andrey_Kuzmin/Shutterstock.com, back cover;   Eric Isselee/Shutterstock.com, back cover

Library of Congress Cataloging-in-Publication Data

Names: Macheske, Felicia, author.
Title: Nifty noses—elephant / Felicia Macheske.
Description: Ann Arbor : Cherry Lake Publishing, 2017. | Series: Guess what |
 Includes index. | Audience: Grades K to 3.
Identifiers: LCCN 2016029427 | ISBN 9781634721769 (hardcover) | ISBN
 9781634722421 (pdf) | ISBN 9781634723084 (pbk.) | ISBN 9781634723749 (ebook)
Subjects: LCSH: Elephants—Juvenile literature.
Classification: LCC QL737.P98 M317 2017 | DDC 599.67—dc23
LC record available at https://lccn.loc.gov/2016029427

Cherry Lake Publishing would like to acknowledge the work of The Partnership for 21st Century Skills.
Please visit *www.p21.org* for more information.

Printed in the United States of America
Corporate Graphics

Table of Contents

My eyes are small for my size.

My ears help me cool off on hot days.

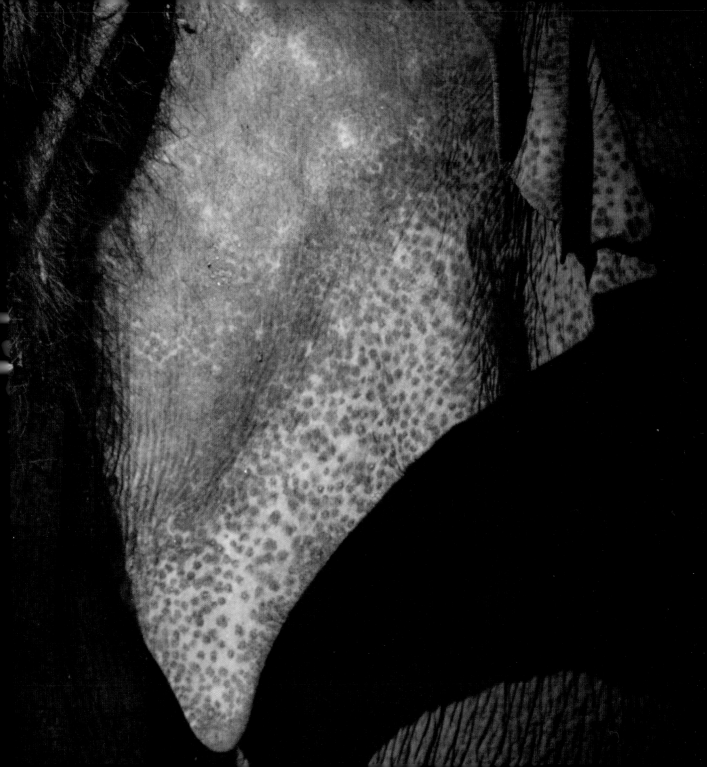

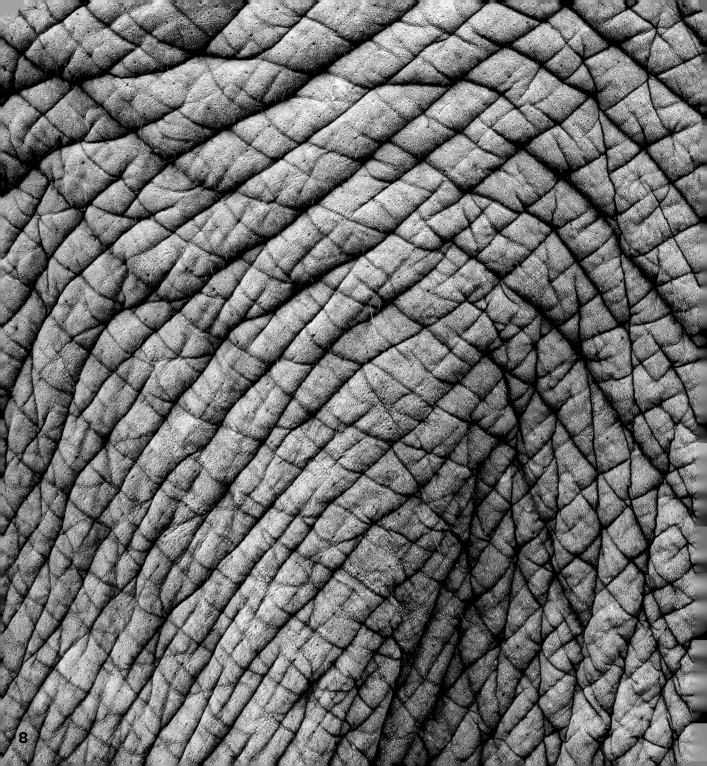

I have thick, wrinkled skin to protect me.

My tusks are really very long teeth.

I have strong legs to carry my large body.

I eat
a lot!

I love to go for a swim when it's hot.

I use my long trunk to grab things.

Do you know what I am?

19

I'm an
Elephant!

About Elephants

1. Elephants use their tusks for many things including digging, removing **bark** from trees, and moving things.

2. An elephant can easily eat up to 300 pounds (136 kilograms) of food a day.

3. Elephants **communicate** with snorts, roars, and some sounds that humans cannot hear.

4. There are two kinds of elephants. They are Asian elephants and African elephants.

5. Asian elephants are **endangered**. African elephants are in risk of becoming endangered.

Glossary

bark (BAHRK) the tough outer covering of trees and other plants

communicate (kuh-MYOO-ni-kate) to share information or feelings with one another

endangered (en-DAYN-jurd) in danger of dying out because of human activity

protect (proh-TEKT) to keep someone or something from getting hurt

trunk (TRUHNGK) the long nose of an elephant

tusks (TUHSKS) the long, curved, pointed teeth that stick out of an elephant's mouth

wrinkled (RING-kuhld) marked with lines in the skin

Index